SEE INSIDE

AN ANCIENT CHINESE TOWN

6407-1

SERIES EDITOR
R.J. UNSTEAD

WARWICK PRESS

Series Editor
R. J. Unstead

Author
Penelope Hughes-Stanton

Adviser
Robert Knox

Editor
Adrian Sington

Illustrations
Charlotte Snook, Mike Saunders
Rob McCaig

Published 1979 by Warwick Press,
730 Fifth Avenue, New York, New York 10019.

First published in Great Britain by Hutchinson
and Co Ltd in 1979.

Copyright © 1979 by Grisewood & Dempsey Ltd.

Printed in Italy by New Interlitho, Milan.

6 5 4 3 2 1   All rights reserved

Library of Congress Catalog Card No. 79-63367

ISBN 0-531-09158-9

CONTENTS

The Town of Loyang	8
A Rich Man's House	10
Clothes and Food	12
Great Inventors	14
Learning and Teaching	16
Working the Land	17
The Market Place	20
Pleasures and Pastimes	22
Defending the Empire	24
Burial Customs	26
Glossary	28
Index	29

FERGHANA

HSIUNG-NU

SOGDIANA

Yellow River · **LOYANG**

Chang-an·

Yangtse River

〜〜〜〜〜 . Great Wall

—————— The 'Silk Route'

—————— Ch'in empire

—————— Early Han empire

—————— Late Han empire

Early China

In AD 25 Loyang became the new capital of the Han empire of China. Ch'ang-an, the old capital, had been destroyed during an uprising. Now, with order restored, Loyang was the center of a civilization that was already highly advanced and which was hardly to change until the present century.

Loyang was built on a tributary of the mighty Yellow River, the cradle of Chinese civilization. People have lived in the river valley for over half a million years. Prehistoric men, of a type known as Peking Man, hunted there for elephants and deer. Then about 4000 years ago, the people of north China learned to farm and so settled in villages. In time, the villages prospered and grew into towns.

The first dynasty (ruling family) about which we know anything very much was the Shang (1500 BC – 1100 BC). Their society was well organized. They had a system of writing and knew how to cast bronze. The emperors governed through a feudal system: the empire was divided into districts governed by loyal rulers who promised to send men to fight for the emperor in return for his protection.

In about 1100 BC the Shang were overthrown by the Chou. But the Chou gradually lost control of the district lords and fighting broke out. The "Warring States" period that followed ended with the victory of the small state of Ch'in. The empire was united, but so harsh was the emperor's rule that, when he died, rebellions raged and the dynasty collapsed.

In 206 BC a peasant leader founded the Han dynasty; and peace was restored. The emperor ruled through officials who were sent to all parts of the empire. After a rebellion in which the capital Ch'ang-an was sacked, the dynasty was to last for 200 years with Loyang as its capital.

Opposite: Bronze models of the massed cavalry that went on the great military expeditions to defend and enlarge the empire.

The Town of Loyang

Loyang occupies a strip of land between the Mang Mountains and the Lo River, from which it takes its name. It lies about 25 kilometers (15 miles) east of modern Loyang. Both river and mountain form good natural protection, but for extra defense a 20 meter-wide (22 yards) stamped earth wall and moat have been built around the town.

You enter the town through one of the gates, some of which are as high as 30 meters (33 yards) and serve as watch towers. The town is laid out on a rectangular pattern, north-south roads being crossed by east-west roads. The square zones formed by this criss-crossing are known as "wards". Each ward is walled and has its own gate, which is closed at night.

The most impressive part of the town is the emperor's palace in the north. It, too, is surrounded by a high wall with massive towered gates wide enough to let carriages through three abreast. The finest houses in the town are to be found near the palace. The poorest people live in the crowded streets near the market places and main gates.

This road is the start of the "silk route" to the west. It leads first to Ch'ang-an, the old capital of the Han empire. From Ch'ang-an, merchants continued their journey across mountains and deserts with silks for the Romans; along the road soldiers marched to keep watch on the Great Wall.

Ron Jobson

To the north, inside the walls of the town, is the burial ground of royalty and officials. The burial mounds you can see are known as tumuli.

Loyang lies between the Mang Mountains and the Lo River. It faces south and is rectangular in shape, measuring two kilometers by three kilometers (one mile by two miles). The town is divided into "Wards". The northern area is occupied by the imperial palace with its granary, stables, temples and pleasure gardens.

A Rich Man's House

This is a house in which an important official in Loyang might have lived. It is surrounded by a wall for privacy. To reach the house itself, you enter through the main gate and cross two courtyards.

The wooden pillars and beams which form the main structure of the house are gaily painted and lacquered (see page 28). The plastered walls of the house are painted with geometric designs. The roofs and tops of the walls are covered with semi-circular pottery tiles. The roof ends are finished off with round tiles decorated with fabulous beasts.

Built into one of the walls is a watchtower from which guards at night keep a constant look out for intruders. In the daytime the women and children sometimes climb the tower to watch the town below.

As you pass into the second courtyard there is a long building on the left. It contains bedrooms and two private sitting rooms, a large one for the master and a smaller one for his wife. In the building straight ahead of you a banquet is taking place. The guests sit on the floor on fur rugs, mats and large colorful cushions. The rooms are richly decorated with silk hangings, painted screens and large bronze urns full of dried flowers. We know the type of houses people lived in from models and pictures found in tombs of this period.

Very rich people might live in houses with three or even four stories and many more courtyards, some with beautiful willows, pine trees and fishponds full of golden carp.

The poor live in narrow crowded streets in cramped shacks with dried mud walls and thatched roofs. In winter they cover the windows with hemp curtains and wrap themselves in thick quilts.

Below: Notice the tiled roofs and the tops of the walls, and also how everything looks inwards.

The poorer families of Loyang live crammed together in homes like this one. The roof is thatched and the walls are made of mud plaster.

Bottom: In the courtyard under the watchtower there is a pigsty. A servant leads a pig to the kitchen on the left where the banquet is being prepared. Other servants carry dishes into the house. In small houses the kitchen might be inside the main building, but here the smell, noise, and dirt are kept well away.

Below: Here you can see the rich furnishings inside the house. The official must be very important to have two guards at the door. On arrival, guests leave their chariots in the front courtyard.

Clothes and Food

The clothes of rich people in Loyang are made of fine silk, often embroidered with complicated patterns. In winter they wear padded clothes and rich furs of badger and beaver.

At court and at religious ceremonies there are strict rules of dress. The shape of the hat, the color of the robe and the symbols embroidered on it all help to show a person's rank. Yellow, for instance, is worn only by the imperial family; and at weddings the more important you are, the more colorful your clothes can be.

As you can see from the banquet scenes (above), the clothes for men and women are much the same: a floor-length, long-

Above: Men and women guests are entertained in different rooms by the host and his lady. They sit on the floor on mats or on little stools. Notice the similarity between the men and women's rich silk robes.

Right: The kitchen, where a banquet is being prepared, is a hive of activity. The rich eat lavishly. Delicacies include turtle, game and dog. A bowl of millet always forms part of the meal. Chopsticks are used to eat with.

sleeved silken robe wrapped round the body and kept in place by a belt or sash.

Men tie their hair up in a knot and cover it with a cloth and hat. (People only cut their hair when in mourning.) Women pile up their hair and decorate it with pins and jewelry. They also wear earrings, bracelets and beautiful belt-hooks. Shoes are made of silk and have wooden soles.

Poor people wear simple tunics made of hemp, tied at the waist. On their feet they wear straw sandals.

The rich of Loyang eat lavishly. They start with a *keng* (stew) of ox, mutton, deer, pig or even dog. This is followed by such exotic dishes as bear's paw, baked owl or panther's breast! Favorite vegetables include bamboo shoots and lotus roots. The meal ends with a bowl of grain food, usually millet, and fruit. Wine, made from grain, is drunk in great quantities.

For the poor there is no such luxury. Most people live on vegetable *keng* and a bowl of millet. Only rarely do they eat meat. From beans and wheat they make bean-curd, noodles and steamed buns.

Above: Fine example of Han dynasty belt-hooks, one in the shape of a tiger, the other of a bird inlaid with turquoise. At first belt-hooks were part of a warrior's outfit; later they were worn every day, but mostly by men.

13

Great Inventors

The emperor's palace and the wealthy houses of Loyang are filled with the fine works of potters, stone-carvers, silk-weavers and lacquer workers. Thousands of skilled craftsmen are needed to provide every kind of luxury from beautiful mirrors with elaborate patterns on the back to bronze vessels and bells, carved jades and delicately shaped and gaily painted pottery.

As well as craftsmen and artists, the empire boasts skilled technicians and inventors, far ahead of their time and rivals. The large picture on the right shows paper being made (paper is one of the great discoveries of the Han dynasty). The raw material is hemp, old silk or mulberry bark. These are things that are easy to get hold of, so making paper is very cheap.

Two of the main industries of the empire are the production of salt and iron. Both are controlled by the government, so as to prevent merchants making large profits from these vital products. Salt is essential to those who live on a grain-based diet, and tools made of iron make life on the land much easier. Also they gave employment to thousands of peasants.

In iron-making large piston bellows are used to increase the heat in the blast furnaces which melt the ore. The molten ore is cast in molds. (It is to be another 1800 years before cast iron is made in Europe.) It is with the tools made from iron that the craftsmen fashion their beautiful objects.

During this Han period there are a number of brilliant physicians who have learned to diagnose and treat diseases, some with herbal medicines; others by *acupuncture*. In acupuncture fine needles are put in certain parts of the human body to control pain. How acupuncture cures ailments remains a mystery, but in China today it is still considered the most effective way to heal people.

Left: Iron-making. Two men operate the huge bellows which raise the temperature in the blast furnaces in which the iron ore is melted. The molten iron then pours into a pan.

Left: Paper-making – one of the many technical achievements of the Han dynasty. The picture shows different stages in the process:
1. Cutting hemp. 2. Mixing hemp with water. 3. Treading the hemp. 4. Making potash from wood. 5. Making a solution from the potash. 6. Straining the mixture. 7. Mixing ash and hemp paste and steaming it. 8 and 9. Pulping the mixture. 10. Stirring mixture in a bath of clean water. 11. Dipping and removing frames from mixture. 12. Drying the frames in the sun.

Above: An hodometer, an instrument for measuring distance traveled by a wheeled vehicle. By means of cogs, after every li (500 meters or 550 yards) traveled one figure strikes the drum, after every ten li traveled the other figure strikes a bell.

Below: A seismograph, an instrument for recording earthquakes, frequent occurrences in China. It was invented by the brilliant Han scientist Chang Heng (AD 78–139). An earthquake tremor causes a vertical pole to tilt against a trigger. This shoots a ball out of the dragon's mouth to the toad below, thus showing the direction of the quake.

SALT FROM THE EARTH

Until the invention of iron, salt could only be made from seawater. With drills made from iron, inland wells as deep as 600 meters (2000 feet) could be bored. Bamboo buckets on long ropes brought the brine (saltwater) up the well. It was then poured into bamboo pipes which carried the water to the stoves, where it was collected in iron pans. The pans were heated over furnaces and the water boiled away leaving salt crystals (a process known as "evaporation"). This salt was stored in hemp sacks near the fire to keep it dry.

Learning and Teaching

The symbol for Yin and Yang, which the Chinese believed were the two great forces in the world. The two forces were opposites. Yang was positive, male, light and warm; Yin was negative, female, dark and cold. A balance or lack of balance of these forces explained everything that happened in the world.

Lao-tze (above) and Confucius.

After the imperial family, the most respected people in Han China are the scholar-officials. Below them come farmers, followed by craftsmen and finally merchants and soldiers. The scholar-officials run the empire, and all education is directed towards training people for this important task.

Intelligent boys are chosen by officials in the provinces and sent to schools in Loyang. There they learn to read and write. This is very difficult and takes a long time, for in Chinese every word has to be learned individually (unlike most languages in which only the alphabet has to be learned). The students also learn mathematics. But the most important part of their education is studying and learning by heart the teachings of Confucius. This philosopher, or thinker, was born in about 551 BC. He believed in order, respect for people of higher rank, and in setting a good example. His golden rule was: 'Do not do to others what you do not want done to you'. In his books you could read short poems and stories; but Confucius did not think up everything that he wrote. Sometimes he would put in a story that some passing traveller had told him.

Any student who does well enough at school and who is considered honest and law-abiding is sent to court for a trial period. If he passes, he may be made an official.

In later dynasties, applicants had to sit several stiff written examinations. The British system for entry into the civil service is copied from the Chinese.

TWO GREAT THINKERS

The Chinese have never had one religion or a single god in which everyone believed. In the early days they worshiped a number of different nature gods and spirits. They believed that everything in nature, particularly such things as mountains, rivers, and winds, had spirits in them. The emperor was go-between for earth and heaven. He offered sacrifices – sometimes human ones – to the spirits so that they would be kind.

The people of the Han empire still believed in these nature gods, but they also followed the teachings of such great teachers as the Buddha (see page 27), Confucius and Lao-tze. Lao-tze and Confucius both lived at about the same time (551 BC–479 BC). Confucius believed that the perfect ruler, one who believed in order and rank, would govern by example. People would so admire him that there would be no need for laws.

Lao-tze's philosophy, Taoism (pronounced Dowism) is very different. Lao-tze taught that the "way" to live cannot be described. People should live by the "principle of nature" and not try to order the world with fixed ideas of what is right and wrong. Some later Taoist masters claimed that they could prolong life for ever. This search for eternal life became a popular cult and several emperors were fooled into believing such claims.

The Taoists have hundreds of gods, ranging from the god of wealth to the god of the kitchen!

Class Night 2014

Mardi Gras

Friday June 6th

Working the Land

Peasant farmers, however poor, had always been highly respected in China. During the Shang and Chou dynasties the peasant had worked for the large landowners, but by the Han dynasty peasants are farming their own land.

The food for Loyang is produced by peasant farmers who live in riverside villages or homesteads outside the town. The illustration above shows a busy springtime scene in a typical homestead. Houses in the villages are sometimes two-storied and have either thatched or tiled roofs. (We know this from earthenware models that have been found in tombs.)

The soil that the farmers till is yellow. In Chinese it is called *huang-t'u* ("yellow earth"). This loess, as we call it, is formed by sand and dust blown by the wind from the deserts of northeast China.

A springtime scene on a farm. It is time for plowing and sowing. To irrigate the land water is raised from the well in buckets and carried on a pole. A more advanced method is the irrigation machine (which you can see in the picture). The machine consists of a chain of scoops operated by pedals. As they turn, the scoops lift water from the pond to the irrigation canals along the fields. Spring is also the time when houses are re-plastered and painted.

17

The Farmer's Year

The main crops in northern China are wheat, millet and hemp. In the south the main crop is rice.

In spring the fields are plowed by ox-drawn plows with iron-tipped shares; sometimes the old type of wooden hand-pushed plow is used. The furrows are then sown with crops and vegetables such as leeks, garlic and cabbages. Lac trees, a type of oak from which lacquer is made, are planted at this time too.

Hemp is harvested in late May. Most people's clothes are made of hemp and its seeds can be eaten when millet is scarce. It grows to over two meters (six feet) tall. It is softened by soaking, a process called "retting", and dried in the sun before the fiber can be separated from the woody stem. The woody stem is used as fuel.

Later in the summer, while the men are hoeing and tending the crops, the women are making silk. The silk comes from moth caterpillars that feed on mulberry leaves.

In fall the harvest is reaped with iron sickles and taken to the granary. The granary is raised on stilts to keep out the damp and rats. The grain is first separated from the husks by threshing. One method uses a treadle which is a simple lever worked by the foot. The "pestle" hammer drops down when the foot is raised and so pounds the grain. The grain is then

Summer on the farm. The peasants are hoeing a field of half-grown millet. Some of the women are busy spinning and weaving silk. It is the women's job to look after the silk worms and to feed them on mulberry leaves. For many hundreds of years the Chinese were the only people who knew how silk is made. Terrible punishments were threatened for anyone who told foreigners the secret of the silk worm.

18

separated from the chaff, or win-
nowed. The grain may be milled
(turned into flour) with a rotary
hand mill. This consists of two inter-
locking furrowed stones. Grain is
poured in through a hole in the top and
ground between the rotating stones.

In winter the farmer rests and mends
his equipment for the next season. If
he has suffered from drought, flood or
a poor harvest, he may have to sell
everything to pay his taxes and work
for someone else.

Each year every male between the
age of 23 and 56 has to spend a month
working for the emperor. He may have
to work on the canals, the Great Wall
or in an iron or salt mine.

*Below: Winter is the time for making and
mending tools, and for resting. But for some it
is time to serve a period of labor for the state.
You can see them being marched off by
officials.*

*Above: In fall the men gather the harvest in buckets and wheelbarrows
and take it to the granary. The women are washing, mending and making
clothes.*

The Market Place

Unlike farmers, merchants are much despised. It is thought shameful to make money from other people, instead of making an honest living from the land. In order to restrict their power the merchants are forbidden to take official posts, and are not allowed to wear silk clothes. Nonetheless many of the merchants of Loyang are very rich, because the market trade is an essential part of town life and has to cater for the needs of the 200,000 people living in the town.

In the market places near the main gates a lively trade is carried on. Through the main gate people are unloading goods from boats on the river. As well as traders from the surrounding countryside there are foreign merchants who have traveled by camel from central Asia.

Near the wall of the market place itself stand two officials who supervise the trading and collect taxes in grain or cash from the stall-holders. All kinds of goods are sold from the stalls – fruit and vegetables, cooked meats, pots and pans, and fine cloths and jewelry. In the market square there is also a public scribe who writes letters or documents for people who cannot write. In the shade of the tree a small group has gathered round a story-teller. One of the most popular people is the soup-seller. As he goes from town to town selling his soup, he passes on local news and gossip. Occasionally there is the gruesome spectacle of a public hanging.

Many luxuries from distant lands are on sale in the market – glass, precious stones, gold and silver from Rome, furs and jade from central Asia. In exchange the foreign merchants return home laden with sumptuous Chinese silks. The gates to the market place are closed at nightfall and reopen at dawn.

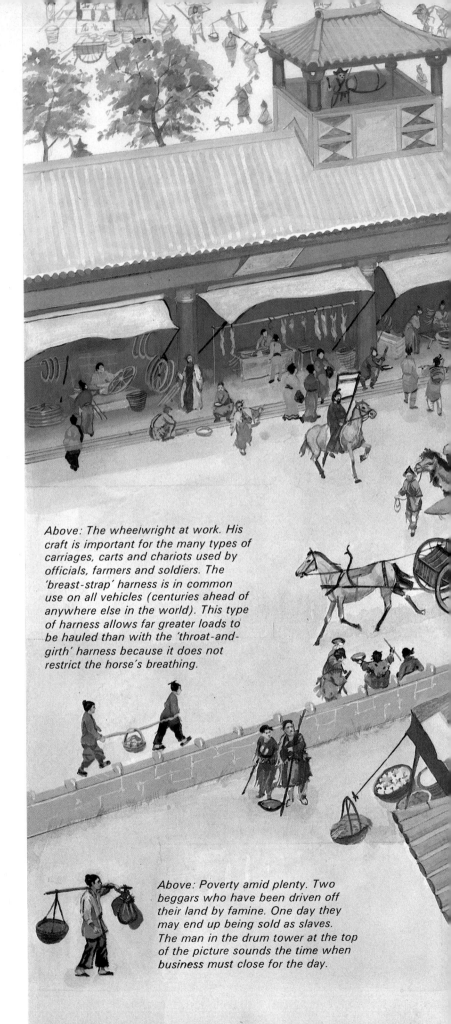

Above: The wheelwright at work. His craft is important for the many types of carriages, carts and chariots used by officials, farmers and soldiers. The 'breast-strap' harness is in common use on all vehicles (centuries ahead of anywhere else in the world). This type of harness allows far greater loads to be hauled than with the 'throat-and-girth' harness because it does not restrict the horse's breathing.

Above: Poverty amid plenty. Two beggars who have been driven off their land by famine. One day they may end up being sold as slaves. The man in the drum tower at the top of the picture sounds the time when business must close for the day.

Above: The market places are near the
main gates and are surrounded by
walls. As well as the strident calls of
stallholders hawking their wares can
be heard the squawks of a cockfight
and the solemn tones of a Buddhist
teacher telling a group of people about
a new religion from India.

Pleasures and Pastimes

The rich people of Loyang spend a great deal of time relaxing and enjoying themselves.

The rich household in the picture on the right has its own troupe of dancers, as well as jesters, acrobats, jugglers and its own small orchestra. The instruments of the orchestra include pan-pipes, called *sheng*, flat stringed instruments, called *ch'in*, drums and beautiful bronze bells which hang on a frame and are struck with a stick. The dancing girls wear colorful, patterned robes. Their hands are covered by long sleeves which flow gracefully as they move.

Most people love to gamble. In one corner a group of people are watching a cockfight. Bets have been laid on the winner. Bullfights are also popular; so too are fights between man and bull. And soldiers often amuse themselves by attaching horns to their heads and having butting contests.

Near the house a group of people are playing a board game called *liu-po* or "sixes". Six bamboo sticks with various markings are shaken and thrown out of a cup. How they land determines where the player moves his counter on the board. Large sums of money can be won or lost at this game.

Flying kites is another popular pastime. Kites were invented in China – mainly for military purposes to send messages. One general of the Han period flew a kite over his enemy's camp and used the cord to measure the length of the tunnel his troops would have to dig in order to reach it.

Below: A model of acrobats entertaining courtiers. It is from models such as these that we know the type of thing people liked to watch and play at in those days.

Outside the house a couple play liu-po while dancers, knife-throwers and musicians perform in the courtyard for a few important officials. In the corner cocks are set to fight and bets are laid on the winner.

Huntsmen set off for the hills in search of deer and wild boar. The emperor has his own hunting parks. His retinue follow him in carriages and on horseback. Imperial huntsmen sport special hats decorated with pheasants' tails and wear pants of white tiger skin. Drums are beaten to flush out leopards, panthers, wolves and bears.

The poor man trudging home laden with fire wood knows little of the pleasures of the big house which the cock-seller has just left.

Defending the Empire

Loyang and other towns of the Han empire are protected from enemy attack by a strong system of defenses. Surrounding Loyang itself is a thick wall and a moat. At the first signal of danger the massive gates to the town are closed and the moatbridge removed. From the multi-story watchtowers, troops prepare to shower the attackers with spears and arrows from their crossbows.

The empire's principal line of defense against foreign invasion is the mighty 2400-kilometer (1500-mile) long Great Wall that stretches along the northern frontiers. In earlier times individual states had built walls along their northern borders to stop repeated invasion from the *Hsiung-nu*, or Huns, a nomadic people to the north and northwest, who lived by herding and hunting. In times of drought or famine the Huns would ride south to pillage food. Unlike the Han people, they were superb horsemen and so the Chinese would try to bribe them with gifts of silk; on one occasion they even sent

Above left: Set into massive walls, one of the main gateways to the town. The drawbridge drops when the bolts are drawn and can be raised again by the attached ropes. The crossbowman and infantryman on the right would have defended the town from the watchtowers, because on the ground they were virtually powerless against the mounted Huns. Below: A cavalryman armed with a long spear.

24

beautiful princesses as wives for their leaders. But at the start of the Ch'in dynasty in 221 BC the emperor ordered thousands of workers to join up the already existing sections of wall. In this way the Great Wall was created. Also at about this time the crossbow was invented. This had a longer range than the Huns' longbows, so that the Chinese were now able to beat them.

Most ablebodied men from Loyang and other cities must spend two years in the army. They receive no pay, but are given food rations, clothing and equipment. The newly enlisted soldiers may be sent to crush a rebellion somewhere in the empire, or they may be ordered on a campaign of conquest to the south or southeast, or to Korea in the north.

Other enlisted men do garrison duty along the Great Wall. The route march from Loyang takes several weeks. Once there the guards have to endure the freezing northern winters, far harsher than the mild climate of Loyang. When not on guard duty, the soldiers are kept busy repairing and improving the wall and the watchtowers in which they are billeted.

This flying horse statue, with its flared nostrils and powerful stride, reflects the awe and admiration the Chinese felt for horses. At first they only had small ponies, but during an invasion they captured some strong, swift Ferghana horses. On these "celestial" or "blood sweating" mounts the heavily armed Chinese soldiers were a match for the invading Huns.

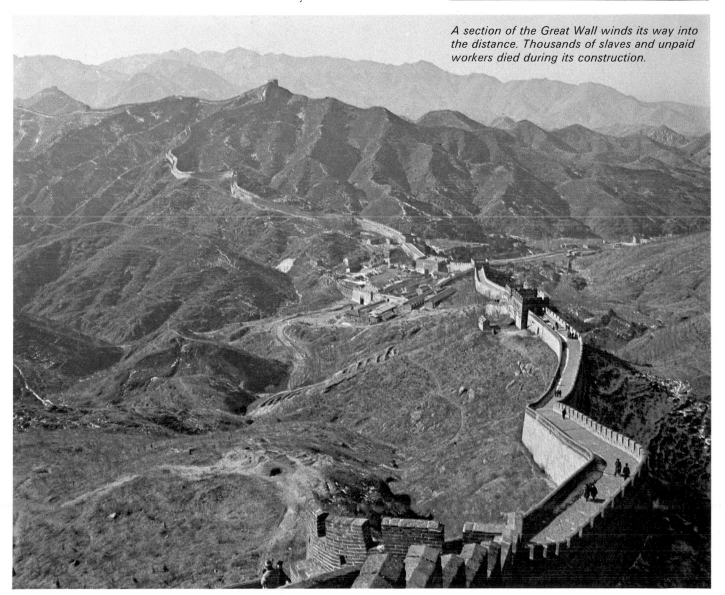

A section of the Great Wall winds its way into the distance. Thousands of slaves and unpaid workers died during its construction.

Burial Customs

In the Shang dynasty, when a king or a member of royalty died, horses and chariots were driven into the grave and slaves and attendants were buried with them. By the Han dynasty, this cruel custom had stopped.

The picture above shows the tomb of Prince Liu Sheng, son of the Han Emperor Ching (157 BC–147 BC). The tomb was discovered in 1968 by soldiers of the People's Liberation Army. In the rear chamber his body lies encased in a beautiful jade suit. The suit is made of 2498 carefully shaped pieces of jade, held together with knots of gold wire. Near the body are sacrificial objects, also made of jade. In the tomb, too, are beautiful bronze vessels and lamps inlaid with gold and silver. In other chambers are buried pottery models of houses, farmyards, animals, cooking stoves and figures of attendants and entertainers. There are pots of wine and food, complete

A reconstruction of the tomb in which Prince Liu Sheng, encased in a jade suit, was buried His wife, Tou Wan, was buried in a similar tomb. Both tombs were hollowed out of the solid rock and filled with huge amounts of treasure and playthings for the dead persons' use in the after-life.

with chopsticks, and even the Prince's chariots and horses. Everything in the tomb is for his use in afterlife.

Death in China was surrounded by all sorts of ceremonies. Everything possible was done to see the dead safely into the next world. The funerals of the rich were very elaborate. Most important was to find the right place for the grave, for it was essential not to upset the earth spirits. If the grave was sited in the wrong spot, bad luck could befall the family.

Huge amounts of money were spent on funerals by those who wished to gain prestige by showing devotion to their parents. The lacquered coffins were placed in a brick vault cut deep into the earth. A mound of earth or shrine would be built on top. The poor could not afford such extravagant funerals and were buried in pits or simple coffins.

These Buddhist statues, near Loyang, were carved out of the cliffs. Each of them is about 50 feet (15 meters) high. You can see the caves dug by Buddhists and which were used as places in which to meditate.

BUDDHISM

Buddhism, one of the world's great religions, reached China from India in about AD 60, during the Han dynasty. At first the Buddhist community in Loyang were mainly foreigners and merchants who had been converted abroad.

Buddhists believe that after you die, you are reborn. If you have led a bad life, you will be reborn in a "lower state" — perhaps as an ant! By giving up "desires", you can escape this rebirth cycle and eventually reach the state of *nirvana* or paradise where you remain for ever.

IMPORTANT HAPPENINGS

c5000 BC New Stone Age. First advanced human beings inhabit Yellow River basin. They had learned to decorate pots and to cut and polish stone.
c2000-1500 BC Legendary Hsia dynasty.
c1500-1027 BC Shang dynasty. Bronze age. First organized society.
1027-771 BC Shang defeated by Chou who came from a province northwest of Loyang; Western Chou dynasty.
771-221 BC Eastern Chou dynasty. The dynasty is divided into two periods:
771-481 BC The Spring and Fall period. Confucius and Lao-tze live in this time.
481-221 BC The Warring States period. The ruling state of Chou is weak and the seven largest states fight among themselves, until the Ch'in defeats them all and unites the empire.
c600 BC First ironworking.
221-206 BC The Ch'in dynasty. Weights, measures and writing are standardized.
213 BC Emperor Shih Huang Ti orders "Burning of the Books". All books but those on practical subjects are burned.
c210 BC The Great Wall established.
206 BC-AD 8 Western Han dynasty. Peasant leader Liu Pang becomes Emperor.
141-87 BC Rule of Emperor Wu ti — regarded as the peak of Han power. His generals expand the empire in all directions.
81 BC Debate on Salt and Iron.
AD 9-23 Wang Mang proclaims his own dynasty, the "Hsin". He fails and peasant rebellions arise led by the "Red Eyebrows" who are loyal to the Han family.
AD 25-220 The Eastern Han dynasty. Emperor Kuang-wu restores the dynasty.
cAD 60 The entry of Buddhism into China from India.
AD 92-192 Period of decline; the imperial family and national army become more powerful than the emperor.
AD 184 Popular rebellions break out. The rebels are known as "The Yellow Turbans".
AD 200 The Three Kingdoms. Three generals proclaim themselves Emperor. This is followed by a very long period of disunity called the "Six Dynasties".
AD 581 The empire is reunited under the Sui dynasty.

CHINESE WRITING

an 'oracle' bone

☉	SUN	日
☽	MOON	月
⋀⋀	MOUNTAIN	山
上 下	UP, DOWN	上 下
一, 二, 三	1, 2, 3	一 二 三
好	GOOD, TO LOVE	好

The characters on the right developed from the original pictograms.
The last character shows how an abstract word has been made from two noun pictograms – "mother" and her "son". Combined, the character means both "to love" and "good".

Writing in ancient China was considered an art. The earliest forms of writing were inscriptions scratched on "oracle" bones used by priests to answer questions. From very early times the writing took the basic form it has today. The system used by the Chinese is based on "characters" or signs. (It is not an alphabet with signs representing different sounds.) Each character stands for a complete idea or thing. The first characters were "pictograms" – simple drawings of such things as the sun, a house, or a tree. More abstract ideas such as the number 3 could be shown as three straight lines. In time the pictures gradually changed, so that by the Han dynasty almost any object or idea could be put into writing. The illustration shows how a few common characters developed from pictograms. Today Chinese writing has over 70,000 characters, although for practical purposes only a few thousand are needed. This writing system has one great advantage: people who speak Cantonese, Hokien or Mandarin Chinese, while not understanding one another's speech, can read the same writing. The characters stand for the meaning rather than the sounds of the words.

Left: A piece of copper 'cash'. The square hole in the middle is for stringing the coins together. Big business was done using gold ingots, which were worth 10,000 coins each. Some goods were bartered – they changed hands in exchange for other goods.

GLOSSARY OF TERMS

BEAN-CURD smooth purée of soya beans which is pressed into cakes.

DYNASTY a family of rulers. It also means the period during which the line of hereditary rulers ruled.

HEMP plant whose fiber is used to make rope and coarse cloth.

HSIUNG-NU name given by the Chinese to the tribes of "Northern Barbarians" who lived beyond the Great Wall.

JADE a very hard stone, green, blue or white in color.

KENG stew made from meat or vegetables.

LACQUER the sap of a kind of oak tree. When heated, the grayish-white molasses turns black. Left in a damp place, it becomes very hard and can be polished until its surface becomes like glass. Pigments can be added.

PICTOGRAMS a picture which is the symbol for a word.

TUMULI mounds of earth built over graves.

INDEX

A
acrobats 22
acupuncture 14

B
banquets 10, 12, 13
board games 22
Buddhism 16, 21, 27
burial customs 26, 27

C
Ch'ang-an 7, 8
Ch'in dynasty 7, 25, 27
chopsticks 12, 27
Chou dynasty 7, 17, 27
clothes 12, 13, 18, 19, 22, 23
    rules of dress 12, 13, 20
Confucius 16, 27
craftsmen 14, 16
crops 17, 18, 19, 28
crossbows 24, 25

D
defense 7, 8, 24, 25
doctors 14
drawbridges 24

E
earthquakes 15
emperor's palace 8, 9, 14

F
farmers 16, 17, 18, 19, 20
farming tools 17, 18, 19
Ferghana 25
food 11, 12, 13, 17, 20, 26, 28
foreign goods 20, 25

G
gambling 22
gates 8, 10, 20, 21, 24
gods 16, 27

government 7, 14, 16, 27
granary 9, 18, 19
Great Wall 8, 19, 24, 25, 27

H
harnesses 20
harvesting 17, 18, 19
hemp 10, 13, 14, 18, 28
hodometer 15
horses 6, 7, 9, 20, 23, 24, 25,
    26, 27
houses 8, 17, 22, 23
    structure of a house 10
Huns 24, 25, 28

I
interior decoration 10, 14, 26
inventions 14, 15, 17, 25
iron-production 14, 15, 19, 27
irrigation 17

J
jade 14, 20, 26, 28
jewelry 13, 20

K
kitchens 11, 12, 13
kites 22

L
lacquering 10, 14, 18, 27, 28
Lao-tze 16, 27
Liu Sheng, Prince 26

M
Mang Mountains 8, 9
market places 8, 20, 21
merchants 8, 16, 20, 21
metal casting 7, 14, 15
money 20, 27, 28
musical instruments 22
    drums 15, 20, 23

P
paper-making 14, 15
pastimes 10, 22, 23
Peking Man 7
philosophers 16, 27
plowing   17, 18
poor people 8, 10, 13, 17, 20,
    23, 27
pottery 10, 14, 20, 26, 27

R
religion 9, 12, 16, 21, 26, 27
rivers 7, 8, 9, 16, 20, 27
    Yellow river 7, 27
Rome 8, 20

S
salt production 14, 15, 19, 27
scholar-officials 16
schools 16
seismograph 15
Shang dynasty 7, 17, 26, 27
silk-making 18
'Silk Route' 7, 8
slaves 20, 25, 26
soldiers 16, 22, 24, 25
state labor   19
story-tellers 20
symbols 12, 16, 27

T
Taoism 16
tomb models 10, 17, 22, 26
tombs 9, 26, 27, 28
town-planning 8, 9

W
wells 15, 17
writing 4, 16, 20, 27, 28

Y
Yin and Yang 16

ACKNOWLEDGEMENTS
Photographs: Endpapers British
Museum; p.7 William MacQuitty;
p.13 British Museum; p.16 Mansell;
p.22 Society for Anglo-Chinese
Understanding; p.25 ZEFA; p.27
Derek Gillman; p.28 British Museum.